CONTENTS

AIN'T NO WAY

Words and Music by
CAROLYN FRANKLIN

DO RIGHT WOMAN DO RIGHT MAN

Words and Music by DAN PENN
and CHIPS MOMAN

CHAIN OF FOOLS

Words and Music by
DON COVAY

DR. FEELGOOD
(Love Is a Serious Business)

Words and Music by ARETHA FRANKLIN
and TED WHITE

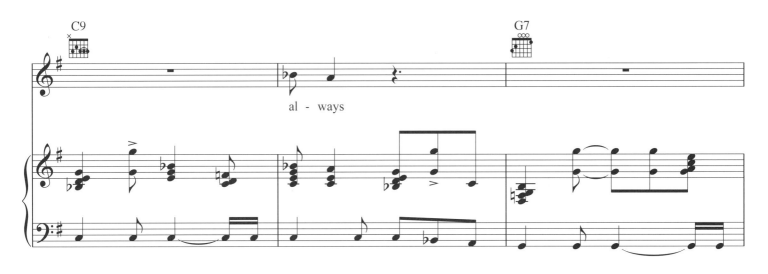

I SAY A LITTLE PRAYER

Lyric by HAL DAVID
Music by BURT BACHARACH

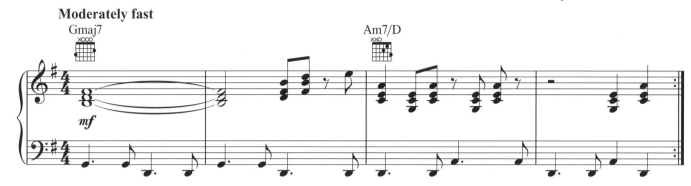

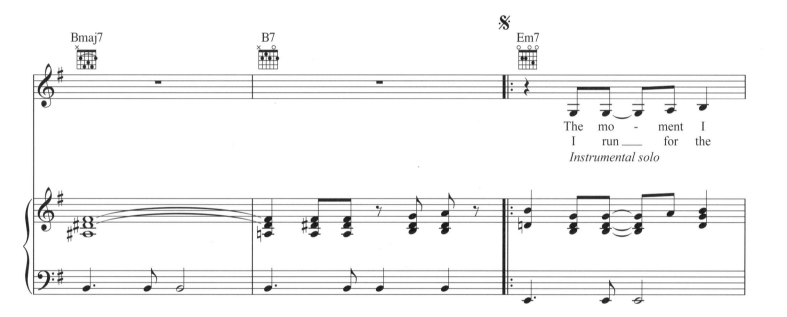

prayer; _____ say ___ you love me, too. _____

Why don't you an-swer my prayer? _____
prayer. _____

Repeat and Fade

Optional Ending

You know, ev-'ry day I say a lit-tle prayer.

HERE I AM
(Singing My Way Home)

Words and Music by JAMIE HARTMAN,
JENNIFER HUDSON and CAROLE KING

* Recorded a whole step lower.

I NEVER LOVED A MAN
(The Way I Love You)

Words and Music by
RONNIE SHANNON

Moderate Blues

(You Make Me Feel Like)
A NATURAL WOMAN

Words and Music by GERRY GOFFIN,
CAROLE KING and JERRY WEXLER

SINCE YOU'VE BEEN GONE
(Sweet, Sweet Baby)

Words and Music by ARETHA FRANKLIN
and TED WHITE

Baby, ba-by, sweet ba-by,

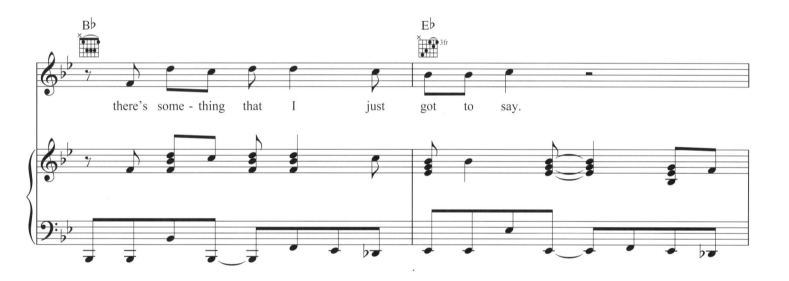

there's some-thing that I just got to say.

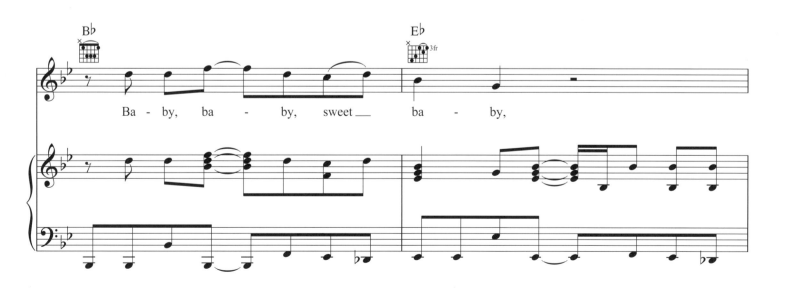

Baby, ba-by, sweet ___ ba-by,

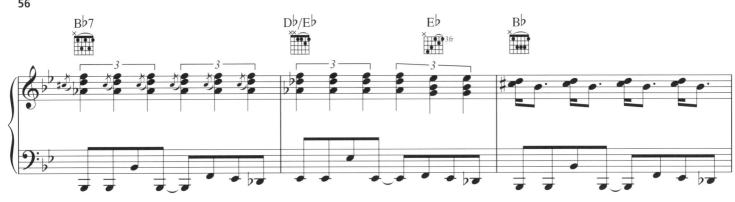

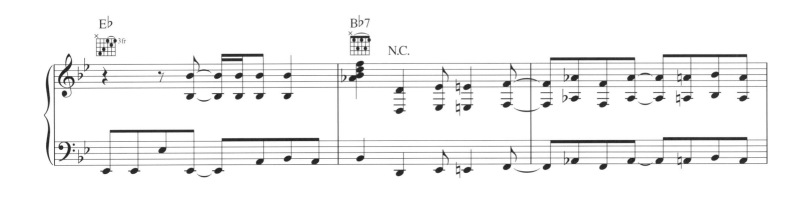

Ba - by, ba - by, sweet

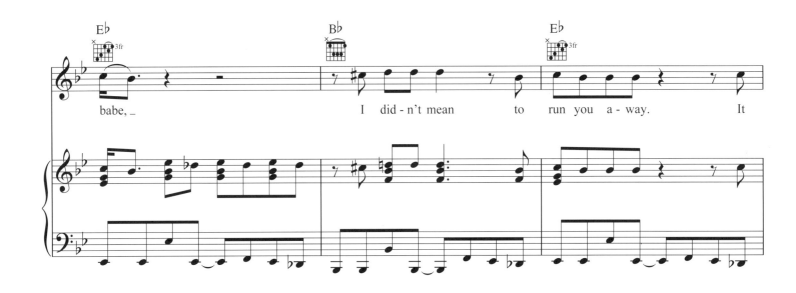

babe, _ I did - n't mean to run you a - way. It

RESPECT

Words and Music by
OTIS REDDING

Moderately fast

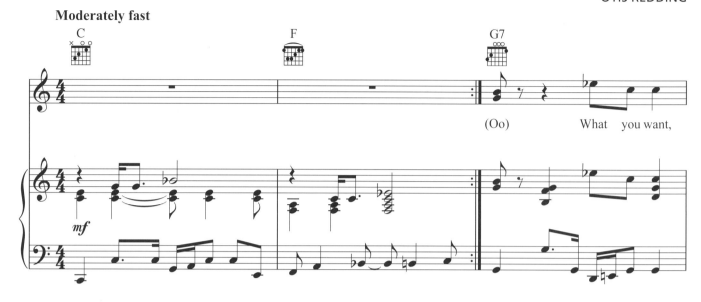

(Oo) What you want,

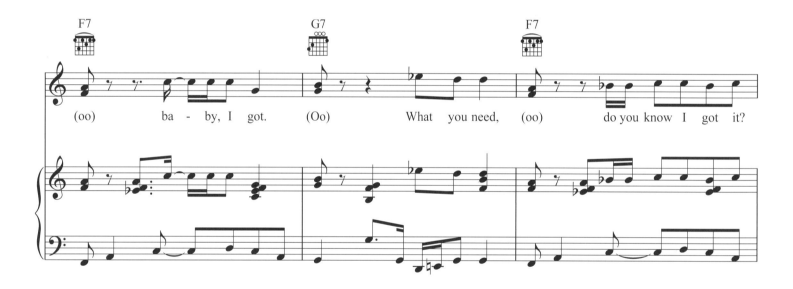

(oo) ba - by, I got. (Oo) What you need, (oo) do you know I got it?

(Oo) All I'm ask - in' (oo) is for a lit-tle re - spect when you come home. Hey,-
(Just a lit - tle bit,)

SPANISH HARLEM

Words and Music by JERRY LEIBER
and PHIL SPECTOR

With a syncopated groove

with eyes __ as black as coal that look down

in his soul __ and start a fi - re there and then __ he los - es con -

trol. And I _____ want to beg __ his __ par -

- don. He's __ go - ing to pick

THINK

Words and Music by ARETHA FRANKLIN
and TED WHITE